Halloween

by Mari C. Schuh

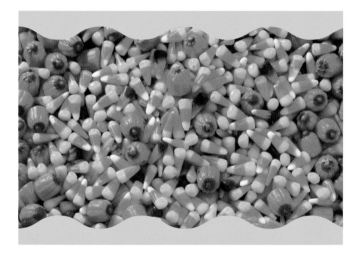

Consulting Editor: Gail Saunders-Smith, Ph.D.

Consultant: Alexa Sandmann, Ed.D.
Professor of Literacy
The University of Toledo
Member, National Council for the Social Studies

Pebble Books

an imprint of Capstone Press
Mankato, Minnesota

Pebble Books are published by Capstone Press
151 Good Counsel Drive, P.O. Box 669, Mankato, Minnesota 56002
http://www.capstone-press.com

1 2 3 4 5 6 07 06 05 04 03 02

Library of Congress Cataloging-in-Publication Data
Schuh, Mari C., 1975–
    Halloween / By Mari C. Schuh.
    p. cm.—(Holidays and celebrations)
    Includes bibliographical references and index.
    ISBN 0-7368-0980-5
    1. Halloween—Juvenile literature. [1. Halloween. 2. Holidays.] I.Title. II. Series.
GT4965 .S425 2002
394.2646—dc21   2001000140

Summary: Simple text and photographs describe the history of Halloween and the
ways it is celebrated.

Note to Parents and Teachers

The series Holidays and Celebrations supports national social
studies standards related to culture. This book describes Halloween
and illustrates how it is celebrated. The photographs support early
readers in understanding the text. The repetition of words and
phrases helps early readers learn new words. This book also
introduces early readers to subject-specific vocabulary words, which
are defined in the Words to Know section. Early readers may need
assistance to read some words and to use the Table of Contents,
Words to Know, Read More, Internet Sites, and Index/Word List
sections of the book.

10,95

Table of Contents

S	M	T	W	T	F	S
		October				
		1	2	3	4	5
6	7	8	9	10	11	12
13	14	15	16	17	18	19
20	21	22	23	24	25	26
27	28	29	30	31		

WITCH WAY

4

Halloween is on October 31.

Halloween began more than 2,000 years ago. Some Europeans celebrated a festival called Samhain on October 31. They lit fires and wore costumes.

The Romans celebrated
a harvest festival in the fall.
This festival and Samhain
became one holiday. The
holiday was later called All
Hallow's Eve or Halloween.

Halloween has many
symbols. A black cat,
a witch, and a ghost
are Halloween symbols.
Black and orange
are Halloween colors.

People carve pumpkins
to make jack-o-lanterns.
They light candles inside
jack-o-lanterns on Halloween.

People visit haunted houses on Halloween.

People wear costumes
on Halloween.

Kids go trick-or-treating on Halloween.

People have costume parties on Halloween. They invite their friends.

Words to Know

harvest—to collect or gather crops

haunted house—a house people visit that is set up to be scary; people often visit haunted houses to celebrate Halloween.

jack-o-lantern—a pumpkin with a face or a design carved into it; people light a candle inside a jack-o-lantern on Halloween.

Roman—a person who lives in Rome; Rome is a city in Italy.

Samhain—a celebration that honors the last harvest of the growing season; some people believed that ghosts visited the earth on Samhain; they lit fires to scare away the ghosts.

symbol—something that stands for something else

trick-or-treating—a Halloween tradition in which children go from house to house asking for treats such as candy

Read More

Klingel, Cynthia, and Robert B. Noyed. *Halloween.* Wonder Books. Chanhassen, Minn.: Child's World, 2001.

Margaret, Amy. *Halloween.* The Library of Holidays. New York: PowerKids Press, 2001.

Rau, Dana Meachen. *Halloween.* A True Book. New York: Children's Press, 2001.

Winne, Joanne. *Let's Get Ready for Halloween.* Celebrations. New York: Children's Press, 2001.

Internet Sites

Absolutely Halloween
http://www.geocities.com/Heartland/7134/Halloween/hall.htm

BrainPOP: Halloween
http://www.brainpop.com/specials/halloween/index.weml

The Halloween Safety Game
http://www.halloweenmagazine.com/play.html

Index/Word List

Word Count: 114
Early-Intervention Level: 15

Credits

Heather Kindseth, cover designer; Kia Bielke, production designer; Kimberly Danger and Deirdre Barton, photo researchers

Capstone Press/Gary Sundermeyer, cover, 1, 10 (upper right, lower left, lower right), 16, 20
Charles Gupton/Pictor, 18
Gary Randall/FPG International LLC, 10 (upper left)
Index Stock Imagery/Kent Knudson, 12
International Stock, 14
MANSELL/TimePix, 8
North Wind Picture Archives, 6
Unicorn Stock Photos/Jim Shippee, 4